1   19 + 26 + 23 = _____

2   685   2,952
  +487   +6,058

3   Number the measurements from largest to smallest.

_____ 3 cm

_____ 3 m

_____ 3 mm

4   What time is $5\frac{1}{4}$ hours after 7:00 p.m.?

_____

5   If one-half cup of popcorn kernels makes two cups of popped corn, how many cups of popped corn will six cups of kernels make?

_____ cups

Show your work.

Daily Math Practice

1   56 – 17 = _____   17 + _____ = 56

2   837   2,315
  – 614   – 748

3   Round 5,294 to the nearest hundred.

_____

4   Mark the **best** description of a square.

○ A square has two sets of parallel sides.
○ A square has four equal angles.
○ A square is a quadrilateral with equal sides and equal angles.

5   Aunt Carol's peanut brittle recipe calls for $\frac{1}{3}$ pound of peanuts per batch. If she makes 8 batches, how many pounds of peanuts will she use?

_____ pounds

1   8 × 7 = _____   80 × 7 = _____

2
$$\begin{array}{r} 9 \\ \times\,2 \\ \hline \end{array}$$
$$\begin{array}{r} 90 \\ \times\ 2 \\ \hline \end{array}$$
$$\begin{array}{r} 90 \\ \times\,20 \\ \hline \end{array}$$

3   Complete the pattern.

1.1   2.2   3.3   _____   _____

_____   _____   _____   9.9

What is the rule?   _____

4   What temperature is 22.7 degrees colder than 96.5 degrees?

_____ degrees

5   A bag of taffy contains three flavors: chocolate, maple, and cherry. There is an equal number of each flavor. What is the chance of reaching into the bag and getting a cherry-flavored piece? Show your answer as a fraction.

_____ chance

1   637 divided by 7 = _____

2 $4\overline{)2{,}876}$

3   Name the shaded part as a fraction and as a decimal.

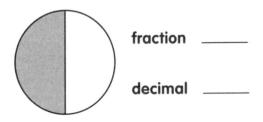

fraction   _____

decimal   _____

4   Write the next three numbers in the pattern.

7   12   17   22   _____   _____   _____

5   Jada spent $43.00 on a new seat and two new tires for her old bicycle. The seat cost $15.00. How much did each tire cost?

$ _____

1. Choose three different digits from 1 to 9. Use those three digits to make all the two-digit numbers you can. Add up the two-digit numbers you created and divide that sum by the sum of the original three digits.

Show your work here.

Write your answer here.

_____

2. Repeat the activity above two more times, using three different digits each time.

Write what you observe about the answers.

_____

1 33 + 52 + 86 = _____

2
  734   2,207
+898   + 1,846

3 Draw all lines of symmetry for the figure below.

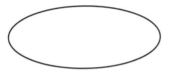

4 How many inches are in 5 feet?

_____ inches

5 Wilbur Wright was born in 1867. His brother Orville was born in 1871. How old was each brother in 1903?

Wilbur   _____ years old

Orville   _____ years old

How much older was Wilbur than Orville?

_____ years older

1 87 − 38 = _____

870 − 380 = _____

2
  398   6,612
− 235   − 4,899

3 Complete the table.

workers	1	2	3	4	5	10	15
hands	2	4	6				

4 Write the first three common denominators of $\frac{1}{3}$ and $\frac{1}{2}$.

_____ _____ _____

5 Mercury is approximately 58 million kilometers from the Sun. Earth is approximately 150 million kilometers from the Sun. How much farther from the Sun is Earth than Mercury?

_____

1 $5 \times 9 =$ _____

$5 \times 900 =$ _____

2
$$\begin{array}{ccc} 30 & 7 & 37 \\ \times\ 8 & \times 8 & \times\ 8 \\ \end{array}$$

3 Continue the pattern.

44 22 88 44 176 88 _____ _____

4 Write the factors of 14. Circle the prime numbers.

_____

5 The Community Council is replanting 6 flower boxes downtown. Each flower box holds 32 petunias. Petunias come in packs of 8 and cost $3.79 per pack. How many packs will the Council need?

_____ packs

Estimate the cost to the nearest dollar.

$_____

1 $50\overline{)350}$ $70\overline{)350}$

2 $2,400 \div 40 =$ _____

3 What place does the **6** have in 764,328?

○ tens
○ thousands
○ ten thousands

4 Write the correct symbol in the circle.

731 ◯ 902

5 The coffee shop has nine apple pies. Each pie is cut into sixths, and each piece sells for $1.50. How much is each pie worth?

$_____

How much are the pies worth altogether?

$_____

1. What number belongs in the shaded block to complete the pattern? _____

Explain how you got that number.

_____
_____
_____
_____
_____
_____

	20	16
12	8	8
7	5	3	5

2. Use the same rule for the pattern above to fill in the empty blocks below.

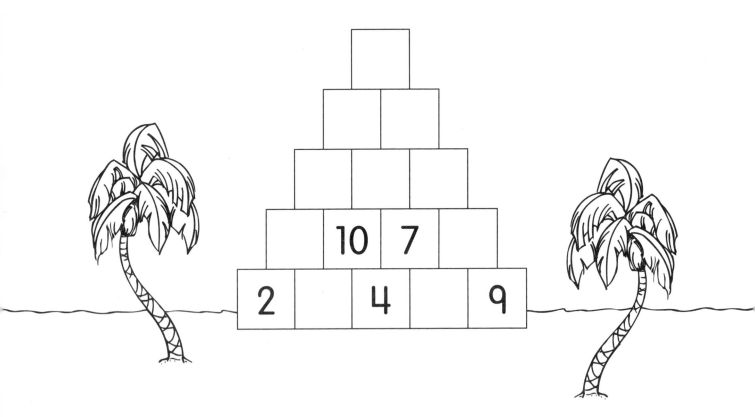

	10	7	
2		4	9

1 36 + 10 + 51 + 49 = _____

2 415   6,217
   +398   +4,983
   ―――   ―――

3 What is the perimeter of a square with 8-inch sides?

_____

What is the area?

_____

4 The temperature on the Fourth of July was 102°F. It was 48 degrees cooler on Thanksgiving. What was the temperature on Thanksgiving?

_____°F

5 Tamara has twelve coins. One-quarter are dimes, one-half are quarters, and the rest are pennies. What is the total value of the coins?

$_____

---

1 783 – 388 = _____

2 85   805   8,005
   – 16   – 106   – 1,006
   ―――   ―――   ―――

3 Write each fraction in simplest form.

$\frac{2}{4}$ _____ $\frac{6}{8}$ _____

$\frac{3}{9}$ _____ $\frac{2}{10}$ _____

4 Which object has the shape of a rectangular prism?

○ pencil   ○ book   ○ scissors

5 The nature museum is open seven days a week. Every day, between 90 and 110 people come to see the exhibits. Mark the best estimate to show how many people come to the museum in one week.

○ 600   ○ 700   ○ 800

1 31 × 5 = _____

2   75   75
      × 4   × 8
     ____   ____

3 If Ben is responsible for mowing 50% of the lawn, what does that mean?

_____

_____

4 If $a = 24$, what is the value of $a + 650$?

_____

5 Mario eats two cups of pretzels every night while he watches television. How many cups of pretzels does he eat in one week?

_____

If there are 13 pretzels in each cup, how many pretzels does Mario eat in one week?

_____

1 2,100 ÷ 3 = _____

2 4)24̄   4)44̄   4)64̄

3 Which is more?

○ one liter
○ one milliliter

4 How many months are in three years?

_____

5 Farmer Frank is planting corn in a three-acre field. He will plant a total of 347 rows with 270 corn plants in each row. How many corn plants will Frank have per acre?

_____ corn plants

➤ Activity 1

Record the attendance for each playoff game on the graph.

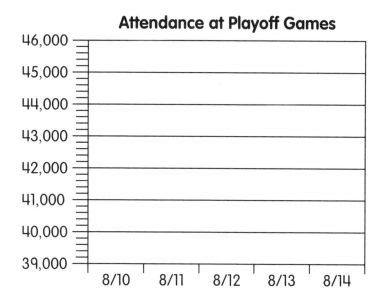

Playoff Games	
Date	Attendance
August 10	42,600
August 11	44,000
August 12	40,800
August 13	45,400
August 14	45,800

What is the total attendance for all five games? (Round to the nearest thousand.) _____

➤ Activity 2

Tyler is moving sand from his driveway to the backyard. The wheelbarrow weighs 30 kilograms when it is full of sand. When it is empty, it weighs 12 kilograms. How many kilograms of sand did Tyler move if he filled and emptied the wheelbarrow five times?

Show your work here.   Write your answer here.

_____

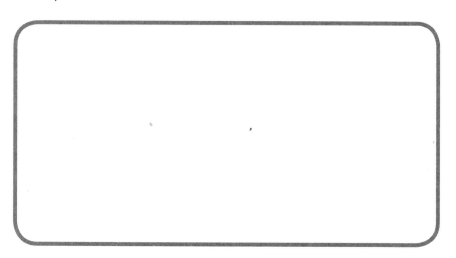

1 391 + 917 = _____

2   4,139
 + 2,524

3 Correct any errors.

1,426 + 2,317 = 3,742

4,138 + 3,522 = 7,663

4 Draw a pentagon.

5 There are 59 boys and 49 girls in this year's baseball league. If the league has nine teams, how many players will be on each team?

_____

Show your work.

1 946 − 266 = _____

2   2,844
 − 1,088

3 Continue the pattern.

▽ ____ ____ ____ ____

4 Mark the **best** description of a decimal point.

○ a dot that means "cents"

○ a dot that takes the place of the word *of* in a number

○ a dot that separates a whole number from a fractional part

5 I am an odd number that is less than 10 and is not the number of sides on a triangle. I can be divided by three. What number am I?

_____

1 506 x 8 = _____

2
```
   12          24
 x 12        x  6
 ----        ----
```

3 Write four equations using the numbers **9**, **7**, and **16**.

_____ _____

_____ _____

4 What place does the **7** have in 187,300?

○ hundreds

○ thousands

○ ten thousands

5 During batting practice, 12 balls were pitched to each player. If 9 players came to practice, how many balls were pitched?

_____

If the players hit an average of 8 balls each, how many balls were hit?

_____

1 810 ÷ 9 = _____

2 3)51̅   3)53̅

3 How many lines of symmetry does a square have?

_____

4 Write the number in standard form.

twelve thousand twenty

_____

5 Kim's new bike cost twice as much as Yoko's. If Yoko's bike cost $189.00, how much did Kim's bike cost?

$_____

Calculate the perimeter and the area for each figure.

1.

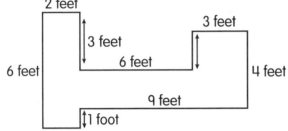

perimeter _____

area _____

2.

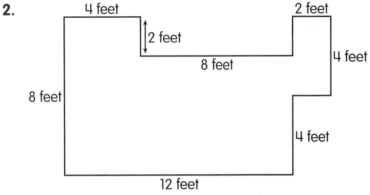

perimeter _____

area _____

3.

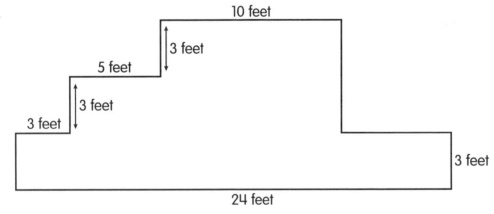

perimeter _____   area _____

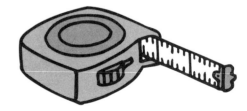

Daily Math Practice • EMC 6715 • © Evan-Moor Corp.

1 19 + 27 + 16 + 24 = _____

2   9,124
  + 6,285
  ‾‾‾‾‾‾

3 What time is 13 hours past 1:00 a.m.?

  _____

4 What is the value of y?

  32 + y = 60 y = _____

5 Every hour on Mondays, the bakers make 75 pies. They make an equal number of pies in each of three flavors: apple, cherry, and lemon. If the bakers work 8 hours on Mondays, how many of each kind of pie do they make that day?

  _____

---

1 262 – 127 = _____

2   4,908
  –   49
  ‾‾‾‾‾

3 Plot the points on the coordinate plane.

  A (4, 1)
  B (–2, 3)
  C (3, 0)

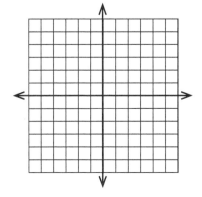

4 How many cups are in a quart?

  _____ cups

5 Ted's patio is the shape of a right triangle.

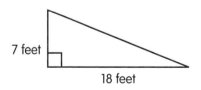

7 feet

18 feet

What is the formula Ted should use to determine the area of the patio?

_____

What is the area? _____

1 9 x 72 = _____

2 0.2 x 4 = _____

0.2 x 5 = _____

3 Write the correct symbol in the circle.

< = >

0.4 ◯ 0.40

0.4 ◯ 4.0

4 Write the equation that shows what 4^3 means.

_____

5 There are 58 stuffed birds in the habitat exhibit. If half of all the birds are from South America, how many South American birds are there?

_____

1 328 ÷ 8 = _____

2

3 List all the factors of 6.

_____

4 Write 705 in expanded form.

_____

5 Earth's diameter is 12,756 kilometers. Saturn's diameter is 120,536 kilometers. The diameter of Venus is 12,104 kilometers. Is the sum of the diameters of these three planets more or less than Jupiter's diameter of 142,984 kilometers?

◯ more   ◯ less

How much more or less?

_____

➤ Activity 1

Mrs. Sage wants to make a book of spelling words for each student in her class. The format of the book is half pages, with a title page, a page for each letter of the alphabet, and an end page. If Mrs. Sage has 70 students, how many reams of paper will she need for the books? (1 ream = 500 sheets)

Show your work here.

Write your answer here.

➤ Activity 2

Fill in the empty squares to make the sum of each row and column equal $2\frac{1}{2}$. Reduce all fractions to simplest form.

1 96 + 93 + 98 = _____

2 649   649
      + 79   +279
      ―――   ―――

3 Write the correct symbol in the circle.

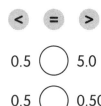

<   =   >

0.5 ◯ 5.0

0.5 ◯ 0.50

4 List all the factors of 10.

_____

5 Carlos got $9.58 for the cans and bottles he recycled, and he earned $18.75 baby-sitting. If he saves $10.50 of this week's allowance, how much money will he have altogether?

$_____

---

1 949 – 325 = _____

2 73,732
      – 36,849
      ―――――

3 What place does the **3** have in 8.3?

○ tens

○ tenths

○ ones

4 Write 132 in word form.

_____

5 Ryan has sixty-eight CDs. He can store fifteen CDs in one CD rack. How many racks does he need?

_____

1 37 x 9 = _____

2 90   92
     x 5   x 5
     ___   ___

3 Continue the pattern.

2 3 5 6 8 ____ ____ ____

What is the rule? _____

4 Which figure is congruent to the shaded one?

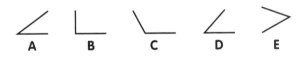

A   B   C   _____

5 Shasha worked in the garden for 3 hours and 40 minutes. She started at 8:30 a.m. At what time did she stop?

_____

1 7)49

2 2)86

3 Number the lengths from shortest to longest.

_____ 1 inch   _____ 10 feet

_____ 1 foot   _____ 1 yard

_____ 10 inches   _____ 0.1 mile

4 Which angles are less than 90°?

∠   ∟   ＼   ∠   ＞
A   B   C   D   E

_____

5 Sudi and Tosha are eating pancakes. If they each can eat one pancake in 3 minutes, how long will it take the two of them to eat 10 pancakes?

_____

➤ **Activity 1**

Continue the pattern and show the rule.

Rule

1. 18 20 22 24 26 _____ _____ _____ | +2 |

2. 84 77 70 63 56 _____ _____ _____

3. 46 49 44 47 42 _____ _____ _____

4. 2 10 5 25 20 _____ _____ _____

5. 10 30 20 60 50 _____ _____ _____

6. 36 40 20 24 12 _____ _____ _____

➤ **Activity 2**

Use the rule to complete the output for each function table.

Rule x6 −3	
Input	Output
4	21
8	
5	
9	
7	
10	

Rule x4 ÷2	
Input	Output
1	2
2	
3	
6	
9	
10	

1 556 + 436 = _____

2   53.7   91.24
  +49.2   +62.85

3 Draw an **X** to show where 5.6 is on the number line.

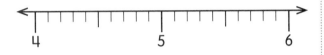

4 Round 106,789 to the nearest ten thousand.

_____

5 Six boys equally divided a bag of candy. Each boy got 3 pieces of taffy, 2 jawbreakers, and 7 lemon drops. How many pieces of candy were in the bag?

_____

---

1 5,473 – 4,266 = _____

2 $\frac{7}{10}$ 361.7
 $-\frac{5}{10}$ – 187.5

3 Use the models below to write a subtraction equation. Show each fraction in simplest form.

_____

4 What are the first four multiples of 4?

_____ _____ _____ _____

5 Mrs. Burns is making cookies. The recipe calls for $3\frac{1}{2}$ cups of flour and $\frac{3}{4}$ cup of sugar. If she wants to double the recipe, how much flour and sugar does Mrs. Burns need?

_____ cups of flour

_____ cups of sugar

1   72 × 6 = _____

2
```
   18        18        18
 × 5       ×10       ×15
 ────      ────      ────
```

3   Number the weights from lightest to heaviest.

_____ 21 ounces

_____ $1\frac{2}{3}$ pounds

_____ 1.5 pounds

4   What is 50% of 76? _____

Show your work.

5   Greg has six nickels, one dime, nine pennies, and two quarters. Parker has a dollar bill. Who has more money?

○ Greg   ○ Parker

How much more? _____

---

1   96 ÷ 6 = _____

2   4⟌616   8⟌616

3   How many minutes are in $2\frac{3}{5}$ hours?

_____

4   What is the volume if each edge of each cube is 1 centimeter?

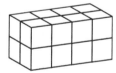

_____

5   Hannah's horse eats 12 pounds of food every day. How much food will Hannah need for the month of January?

_____

➤ **Activity 1**

Write each value in the correct place to show the number.

1. 6 ones
3 ten thousands
0 hundreds
9 tens
4 thousands

_____34,096_____

2. 5 tens
0 thousands
7 ones
2 ten thousands
1 hundred

_____

3. 8 hundreds
0 ten thousands
2 tens
0 ones
0 thousands

_____

4. 6 thousands
3 tens
5 hundreds
2 ones
7 ten thousands

_____

5. 0 ten thousands
1 hundred
3 ones
6 thousands
0 tens

_____

6. 9 tens
0 ones
9 thousands
4 ten thousands
0 hundreds

_____

➤ **Activity 2**

Use the clues and the grid to determine which present each child received.

Clues

- James did not get the present in the green box.

- Maya's present was in a box that is the same color as her bunny's nose.

- The color of the box for Brett's present begins with the same letter as his name.

	blue	green	pink	white
James				
Maya				
Brett				
Elisa				

1 587 + 239 = _____

2 8,236
+ 1,537

3 Complete the table.

fraction	decimal	percent
$\frac{1}{4}$	0.25	
	0.1	10%
$\frac{2}{5}$		40%
$\frac{1}{2}$		

4 Write each fraction in simplest form.

$\frac{9}{24}$ _____ $\frac{12}{60}$ _____

5 Luis is 12 inches shorter than Eva. Eva is 3 inches taller than José. If José is 48 inches tall, how tall are Eva and Luis?

Eva _____ inches

Luis _____ inches

1 3 − 0.5 = _____

2 $\frac{3}{4} - \frac{1}{4}$ = _____

3 Each block in the figure represents one cubic unit. Write and solve the equation to find the volume of the figure.

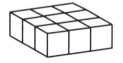

_____

4 What is the surface area of the figure in problem 3?

_____

5 Mira found 16 pennies, 4 nickels, 3 dimes, 6 quarters, and 2 one-dollar bills in her purse. How much money does she have?

$_____

1 85 x 7 = _____

2
```
  34        34        34
x 20      x 21      x 22
----      ----      ----
```

3 Write the equation to find the perimeter of the equilateral triangle.

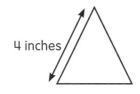

4 inches

_____

4 Mark the **best** definition of a quotient.

○ the answer to a multiplication problem
○ the answer to a division problem
○ the number to be divided

5 Mrs. Watson's jar of beads contains 100 red beads, 50 blue beads, and 50 green beads. If she pulls out a bead without looking, what is the chance that the bead will be blue?

○ 25%   ○ 33%   ○ 50%

1 95 ÷ 5 = _____

2 4)2,400   6)2,400

3 Continue the pattern.

○ ▽ ◇ ○ | ○ ▽ ◇ _____

_____ _____ _____ _____

4 What are the common factors of 10 and 5?

_____

5 Karl stacked twelve 1-inch cubes in three layers on top of a square made with four 1-inch cubes. What shape is the structure that Karl made?

○ pyramid
○ triangular prism
○ rectangular prism

Use the formula $V = l \times w \times h$ to calculate the volume of each box.

1.

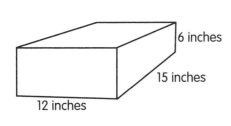

6 inches

15 inches

12 inches

_____

2.

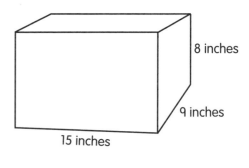

8 inches

9 inches

15 inches

_____

3.

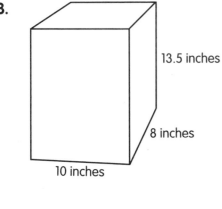

13.5 inches

8 inches

10 inches

_____

4.

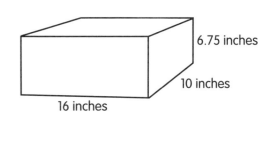

6.75 inches

10 inches

16 inches

_____

What conclusion can you draw about the boxes?

_____

_____

1   62.5 + 49.7 = _____

2   68,412
   +53,978

3   Circle the numbers that are divisible by **5**.

      370   501   865   720

    4,385   22,463   793,440

4   Round 4,379,821 to the nearest hundred.

    _____

5   Polly the parrot has learned to say "Polly wants a cracker." If she says it every five minutes for two hours and gets a cracker to eat each time, how many crackers will Polly eat?

    _____

1   32.04 − 10.42 = _____

2   63,947
   −29,185

3   Write the fractions for points **A** and **B** on the number line.

A _____   B _____

4   What is $\frac{1}{2}$ of 84?   _____

What is 50% of 84?   _____

5   Farmer McDonald is building a fence around his pasture. He is placing posts 6 feet apart and will stretch wire between them. If the pasture is 36 yards long and 14 yards across, how many posts will Farmer McDonald need?

    _____

1 128 x 8 = _____

2
$916\frac{1}{10}$ 916.1
x   4   x   4
_____   _____

3 Write the correct symbol in the circle.

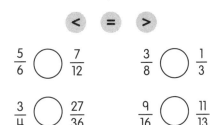

< = >

$\frac{5}{6}$ ◯ $\frac{7}{12}$ $\frac{3}{8}$ ◯ $\frac{1}{3}$

$\frac{3}{4}$ ◯ $\frac{27}{36}$ $\frac{9}{16}$ ◯ $\frac{11}{13}$

4 Circle four and six tenths.

4.06   46   4.6   64

5 Caleb made a stack of popcorn balls on a table. He placed sixteen balls on the table, then added three more layers on top of them. Each layer had four fewer balls than the previous layer. How many popcorn balls in all were in the stack?

_____

1 924 ÷ 12 = _____

2 6)3,858

3 Write the expression.

Add thirty-eight and fifty-two, then divide by four and a half.

_____

The answer is _____.

4 What is the area of a rectangle that measures 8 inches by 23 inches?

_____

5 In the class election, 46% of the students voted for Selina. If there are 50 students in the class, how many votes did Selina get?

_____

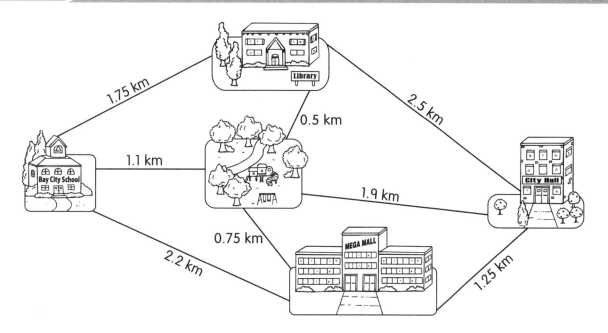

Trisha walked from school to the library and then to the park. Jennie ran from the park to the shopping mall and then to City Hall. Alexis walked from school to the park, then to the library, and finally, back to school. Madison rode her bike the entire perimeter of the area shown on the map.

Use the map to answer the questions.

1. Which girl traveled the farthest?

○ Trisha   ○ Jennie   ○ Alexis   ○ Madison

2. Is the combined distance traveled by the other three girls more or less than the girl who traveled the farthest?

○ more   ○ less

How much more or less? _____

3. What is the total distance traveled by all four girls? _____

Work Space

1 $3\frac{1}{8} + 2\frac{1}{2} =$ _____

2 $\begin{array}{r} 10{,}985 \\ +\ 2{,}785 \\ \hline \end{array}$

3   Write the percent form of each fraction.

$\frac{1}{2}$ _____ $\frac{7}{10}$ _____

$\frac{3}{4}$ _____ $\frac{4}{5}$ _____

4   What is the least common multiple (LCM) of 6 and 10?

_____

5   Draw and label a Venn diagram that shows the intersection of the sets below.

Set A = 2, 4, 6, 8, 10
Set B = 5, 10, 20, 30, 40

1 $6\frac{7}{10} - 3\frac{2}{5} =$ _____

2 $\begin{array}{r} 495{,}783 \\ -\ 62{,}016 \\ \hline \end{array}$

3   What is the chance, or probability, of spinning a **3**?

○ 1 in 6

○ 2 in 3

○ 1 in 3

4   Simplify the expression $(6 \times 2) - 4$.

_____

5   What is the average score per game?

Game	Points
1	69
2	48
3	57
4	70
5	66

_____

1 $35\frac{1}{2} \times 5 =$ _____

2
$$\begin{array}{r} 35.5 \\ \times \quad 5 \\ \hline \end{array} \qquad \begin{array}{r} 355 \\ \times \quad 5 \\ \hline \end{array}$$

3   If Olivia buys six 12-packs of fruit snacks for $14.40, how much does each fruit snack cost?

$ _____

4   Write the number in standard form.

one hundred six thousand forty

_____

5   Complete the table and explain the rule.

Input	Output
2	4
3	9
4	16
5	
6	
7	

_____
_____
_____
_____

1 $810 \div 9 =$ _____

2 $64\overline{)1,600}$ $64\overline{)3,200}$ $64\overline{)4,800}$

3   Mark the units that measure length.

   ○ hectogram   ○ millimeter
   ○ kilometer   ○ deciliter
   ○ centimeter   ○ kilogram

4   How many lines of symmetry does the figure have? Draw it.

   ○ 0   ○ 2
   ○ 1   ○ 3

5   Elijah is planning a picnic. He will invite twice as many boys as girls. If he invites 18 people, how many boys and how many girls will get invitations?

boys _____   girls _____

➤ Activity 1

Wyatt is painting boxes that are stacked one on top of the other. He paints only the sides (not the top or bottom) of each box. He will, however, paint the top of the box at the very top of the stack. Complete the function table to show how many faces Wyatt will paint on each stack of boxes.

Number of Boxes	Faces to Paint
3	
5	
8	
11	

What is the rule? _____

➤ Activity 2

Complete the function tables.

Input	Output
2	15
3	25
	55
9	
13	
22	215

What is the rule? _____

Input	Output
12	10
	16
32	
62	35
70	39
86	

What is the rule? _____

1   6.54 + 8.31 = _____

2   118,643
   + 97,968

3   If two angles of a triangle each measure 45 degrees, what kind of angle is the third angle?

     ○ acute   ○ right   ○ obtuse

4   If the sum of two numbers is 24 and the product is 140, what are the two numbers?

     _____ and _____

5   Cam collected twenty-five soda cans. Five of the cans are root beer cans. What percent of Cam's cans are root beer cans?

     _____

1   9.47 – 0.37 = _____

2   652,267
   +288,912

3   Write the correct symbol in the circle.

     –4 ◯ –6

     0.2 ◯ –1.2

4   Write the value of **8** in 1,386,672 in word form.

     _____

5   Trevor is $8\frac{1}{2}$ inches shorter than his dad. If his dad is $6\frac{1}{4}$ feet tall, how tall is Trevor?

     _____

     Show your work.

1 $6\frac{1}{3} + 8\frac{1}{4} =$ _____

2
$$
\begin{array}{r}
280.1 \\
\times \quad\ 6 \\
\hline
\end{array}
$$

3   How many rectangular faces does a triangular prism have?

     ○ 3   ○ 5   ○ 6

4   Write the number below in standard form.

     one thousand six and six tenths

     _____

5   Lisa and Rachel baby-sat three children for five hours. If they were paid $2.50 per hour for each child and divided their earnings equally, how much did each girl receive?

     $_____

1 $4.9 \div 7 =$ _____

2 $15\overline{)1,230}$

3   Write the decimals for points **A** and **B**.

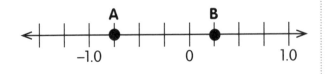

     A _____   **B** _____

4   Is an oval a polygon?

     ○ **yes**   ○ **no**

5   Penny compared the price of gumdrops at two stores. At Save-More Market, gumdrops are $3.95 per pound. At the Buy-Here Warehouse, the price is two pounds for $6.50. Which store has the better buy? Explain your answer.

     _____

     _____

     _____

Make a graph to show the information in the table. (Remember to complete the key and to include axis labels and a title on your graph.)

Goals Scored		
	Home Team	Opponents
Game 1	4	2
Game 2	3	1
Game 3	1	5
Game 4	6	3
Game 5	2	6

Key

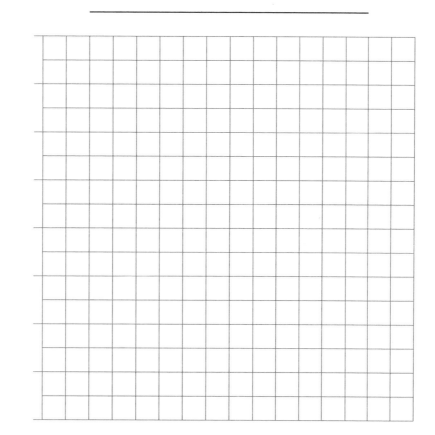

1 $22\frac{3}{4} + 33\frac{1}{3} =$ _____

2   789,321
     –   2,989

3 Which figures are congruent?

   A   B   C   D   E

_____

4 Write 352.8 in expanded form.

_____

5 David is saving money to buy a new computer game. The game costs $39.99. He has saved $27.14. How much more does he need?

    $_____

---

1 $87.62 – 48.95 =$ _____

2   6
     $-2\frac{1}{2}$

3 What is the volume?

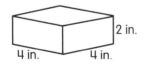

2 in.
4 in.   4 in.

_____

4 What is the greatest common factor (GCF) of 6 and 9?

    _____

5 The temperature on a cold December morning dropped from 37° to –4°. How many degrees did the temperature fall?

    _____

1 757 x 30 = _____

2 3.9
     x 2.3
     ‾‾‾‾

3 Mrs. Diaz wants new carpet for her living room. The room is 15 feet by 12 feet. How many square yards of carpet will Mrs. Diaz need?

_____

4 If the price of the carpet in problem 3 is $15.99 a square yard, how much will Mrs. Diaz have to pay for new carpet in her living room?

$_____

5 Continue the pattern.

2 5 3 5 4 5 _____ _____ _____

---

1 $60 \div \frac{1}{2}$ = _____

2 $30\overline{)15.90}$

3 Draw the cone shape below when it is slit from the edge to the center point and flattened out.

4 10% of 20 = _____

Show your work.

5 Jana and Anthony walk home from school on Monday, Wednesday, and Friday. Their mother picks them up on Thursday, and they ride the bus on Tuesday. What fraction of the time do they walk home from school?

_____

The Lowe family always orders a two-topping pizza. List all the combinations they can make with the toppings below.

Pizza Toppings

black olives
green peppers
onions
pepperoni
sausage

_____   _____

_____   _____

_____   _____

_____   _____

_____   _____

_____   _____

How many different two-topping pizzas can the Lowes make? _____

1   37 + 26.55 = _____

2   84,320
  +16,791

3   What solid figure will this flat pattern form when it is folded?

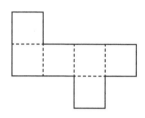

    ○ pyramid   ○ cone   ○ cube

4   Circle the prime numbers.

     2   92   59   6   5   12

5   A motorcyclist used 3.21 liters of gasoline, traveling from Greenfield to Milltown. The next day, he used 1.95 liters going from Milltown to New Haven. Approximately how much gas in all did he use?

    ○ about 3 liters   ○ about 5 liters
    ○ about 4 liters   ○ about 6 liters

---

1   324 – 192 = _____

2 $\frac{3}{4}$ $\frac{3}{8}$

   $-\frac{1}{8}$ $-\frac{1}{4}$

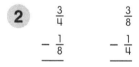

3   Write the number in standard form.

four hundred five thousand three hundred sixty-six

_____

4   Reduce $\frac{6}{8}$ to simplest form.   _____

5   During the candy sale, the three students in Matt's group raised a total of $732.53. Bob sold $232.46 worth of candy. Cathy sold $189.21. How much did Matt sell?

      $_____

1 64 x 180 = _____

2　$11\frac{1}{2}$
　　$\times\ \ 3$
　　‾‾‾‾‾

3 Simplify and solve the expression.

$$(16 - 8) + 5$$

_____

4 Write the next three numbers in the pattern.

2　8　32　_____　_____　_____

5 Mrs. Black has one begonia plant. If she buys two begonia plants each year for every plant she has, how many begonia plants will she have in all after four years? Complete the function table to show your answer.

years	0	1	2	3	4
plants	1				

1 $\frac{1}{5} \div 2 =$ _____

2 $48\overline{)1,632}$

3 Round 308.61 to tenths.

_____

4 Write the letters for each part of the circle next to the correct label.

diameter _____

center _____

radius _____

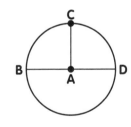

5 Our class donated $1.50 per student to the city's park project. The total donation was $52.50. How many students are in our class?

_____

Daily Math Practice • EMC 6715 • © Evan-Moor Corp.

Zack took four math tests each semester this school year. Each test was worth 100 points. On the first test in the first semester, he got a score of 85. On the second test, he scored 92. He earned 70 points on the third test and 96 points on the last test. During the second semester, Zack scored 82 on the first test, 95 on the second test, 90 on the third test, and 86 on the last test.

Complete a double line graph to show Zack's test scores.

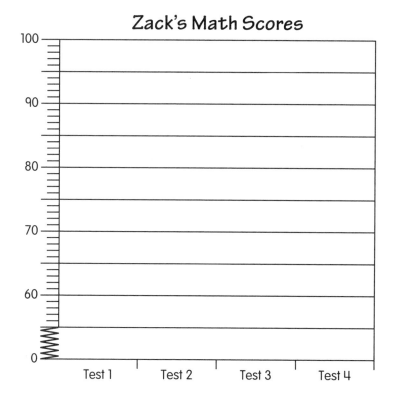

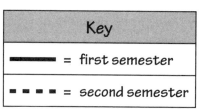

Use the graph to answer the questions.

1. What was Zack's average test score in math for the school year? _____

2. In which semester did Zack earn the higher average test score?

     ○ first semester   ○ second semester

3. What was Zack's median math test score for the year? _____

WEEK 14 DAY 1 Daily Math Practice

1 18.2 + 17.6 + 42.3 = ________

2 $\frac{8}{9} + \frac{1}{3}$ $\frac{8}{9} + \frac{4}{12}$

3 What shape is the base of a cube?

○ triangle
○ square
○ rectangle

4 Round 894,754,390 to the nearest million.

____

5 The chart below shows Emily's savings account balance. If she continues to save at this rate, how much money will she have at the end of eight weeks?

Week	Account Balance
1	$2.00
2	$3.50
3	$5.00

$________

WEEK 14 DAY 2 Daily Math Practice

1 $66\frac{1}{2} - 43 =$ ________

2 10,000 − 47

3 What is the least common multiple (LCM) of 3, 7, and 6?

____

4 A good estimate for 702 x 43 will contain how many digits?

○ 3 ○ 4 ○ 5

5 Mia, Lee, Will, and Tay compared their math scores: 100, 99, 92, and 86. Use the clues below to match the students with their scores.

- Mia scored higher than Will but lower than Tay.
- Lee's score was higher than Will's but lower than Mia's.

100 ________ 99 ________

92 ________ 86 ________

1   0.53 × 0.27 = _____

2 $\frac{3}{5}$ $\frac{9}{15}$

    × $\frac{3}{10}$ × $\frac{9}{30}$

3   What is the surface area of a 3-inch cube?

    _____

4   9 : 3 :: 49 : _____

5   Steve does in-line skating for exercise. He skates 4 kilometers on Mondays, 5 kilometers on Thursdays, 8 kilometers on Saturdays, and 10 kilometers on Sundays. If he skated a total of 17 kilometers one week, on which days did he skate?

    ○ Monday   ○ Thursday

    ○ Saturday   ○ Sunday

---

1 $\frac{1}{10}$ ÷ 3 = _____

2   6)4,410   6)44.10

3   Mark the **best** description of a square.

    ○ A square is a polygon.

    ○ A square is a quadrilateral.

    ○ A square is a plane figure.

4   The average of four numbers is 21. If three of the numbers are 12, 18, and 28, what is the missing number?

    _____

5   Caramel apples cost $2.00 each. Nuts and chocolate sprinkles each cost 50¢ extra. Tessa wants a caramel apple with nuts. Chelsea wants both nuts and sprinkles. Max wants his caramel apple plain. How much will the three apples cost altogether?

    $_____

➤ **Activity 1**

Round the answers to the nearest hundredth.

8)1.63   6)3.65   4)7.25   7)8.99

➤ **Activity 2**

The frozen yogurt shop sells cones in five different sizes.

Yogurt Cones		
Size		Price
Baby	3 ounces	$0.75
Small	5 ounces	$1.35
Regular	8 ounces	$2.25
Large	12 ounces	$3.60
Giant	16 ounces	$4.20

Look at the sign. Which size yogurt cone is the best buy?

○ Baby   ○ Small   ○ Regular   ○ Large   ○ Giant

Work Space

1   2,804 + 9,782 = _____

2   18,706
    + 3,897

3   If you place six equilateral triangles side by side so that two sides of every triangle touch one of the other triangles, which shape will you form? Draw the shape.

    ○   pentagon

    ○   hexagon

    ○   octagon

4   What is the largest number you can make with the digits 0, 2, 8, and 9?

    _____

5   The highway patrol officer's radar clocked cars traveling at 75 mph, 65 mph, 64 mph, and 70 mph. What was the average speed?

    _____

---

1 $93\frac{1}{2} - 72\frac{1}{4} =$ _____

2   97,000
    − 3,529

3   List all the factors of 28.

    _____

4   What are the first three prime numbers?

    _____   _____   _____

5   Liam and his dad are repairing the railing on their deck. They put up eight supports with 4 feet between each one. If the first support is at one corner of the deck and the eighth support is at the other corner, how long is the side?

    _____

1 189.45 x 8.6 = _____

2 $\frac{3}{4}$ $\frac{12}{16}$

 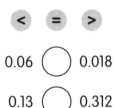

3 Write the correct symbol in the circle.

< = >

0.06 ◯ 0.018

0.13 ◯ 0.312

4 How many ounces are in 4 pounds?

_____

5 An inchworm crawling up a branch climbed 100 centimeters the first hour, 90 centimeters the second hour, and 80 centimeters the third hour. At this rate, how many centimeters will it have climbed after 5 hours?

_____

1 $3\frac{1}{2} \div 7 =$ _____

2 $75\overline{)8,605}$

3 Which is greater?

○ 66 x 6   ○ 94 x 4

4 Is a circle a polygon?

○ **yes**   ○ **no**

5 Mark solved 18 out of 20 problems correctly on his math quiz. What percent of the problems were correct?

_____

Show your work.

1. Choose three **different** digits from 1 to 9.   ____ ____ ____

   Use the digits to make the largest and smallest numbers you can.   _____ _____

   Subtract the smallest number   Copy the difference.
   from the largest number.   Then reverse its digits and add.

   _____ largest number   _____ difference

   − _____ smallest number   + _____ difference reversed

   _____ difference   [   ] sum

2. Repeat the steps above using three other digits.

   _____   _____
   − _____   + _____
   _____   [   ]

3. Try it with four different digits.

   _____   _____
   − _____   + _____
   _____   [   ]

   How did the sum change, using four digits instead of three?

   _____

   _____

4. Will the same thing happen using five digits?   ○ **yes**   ○ **no**

   Try it!

   _____   _____
   − _____   + _____
   _____   [   ]

1 120 + 792 = _____

2 763,199
  + 3,672
  _____

3 Calculate the perimeter (**p**) and the area (**a**).

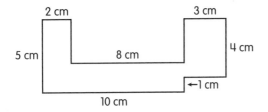

p = _____

a = _____

4 What is the value of *a* in the equation
3 x *a* = 24?

a = _____

5 Max spent a total of $72.77 at the clothing store. He paid with four $20 bills. What change did he receive if the clerk gave him the fewest possible number of coins and bills?

_____

_____

1 97,203 − 59,868 = _____

2 503.69
  − 20.01
  _____

3 Write the correct symbol in the circle.

< = >

$\frac{5}{6}$ $\frac{7}{8}$ $\frac{5}{25}$ $\frac{1}{5}$

$\frac{3}{4}$ ◯ $\frac{2}{3}$ $\frac{1}{4}$ ◯ $\frac{1}{3}$

4 Is a sphere a solid figure?

◯ **yes**   ◯ **no**

5 Clovertown students attend school five days a week for thirty-six weeks each school year. A school day is six hours long. How many hours do the students spend in school each year?

_____

1. $0.37 \times 9.6 =$ _____

2.
$$\frac{1}{2} \qquad \frac{21}{42}$$
$$\times \frac{6}{7} \qquad \times \frac{36}{42}$$

3. Two intersecting lines are parallel.

   ○ **yes**   ○ **no**

4. Circle the digit that is in the tenths place.

   ### 145.6

5. Ella bought a pizza for dinner. On the way home, she ate $\frac{1}{8}$ of the pizza. Her brother ate $\frac{1}{4}$ of the pizza while he was setting the table. How much pizza was left for dinner?

   ○ $\frac{3}{4}$ ○ $\frac{3}{8}$ ○ $\frac{5}{8}$

1. $210 \div \frac{1}{5} =$ _____

2. $12\overline{)7.32}$

3. Draw an obtuse angle.

4. Which number is forty-five thousand three hundred sixty-six?

   ○ 4,536   ○ 405,366
   ○ 45,366   ○ 4,530,066

5. In Rosa's class, there are 15 boys and 12 girls. On Wednesday, all the girls were present and $\frac{1}{5}$ of the boys were absent. How many students were in class that day?

   _____

➤ **Activity 1**

Write a word problem for the answer **6 boxes of 12**.

_____

_____

_____

_____

➤ **Activity 2**

How many facts can you complete in one minute?

9 +5	7 +3	6 +6	8 +1	4 +2	6 +8	5 +7	8 +4
6 −3	12 − 8	9 −4	15 − 1	18 − 7	8 −2	16 − 0	7 −6
7 ×8	6 ×6	9 ×3	8 ×5	12 × 0	2 ×1	4 ×11	12 × 6

$9\overline{)81}$ $7\overline{)35}$ $6\overline{)48}$ $5\overline{)55}$ $4\overline{)28}$ $8\overline{)16}$ $3\overline{)21}$ $1\overline{)15}$

_____ correct

1 $75\frac{1}{4} + 82\frac{1}{4} = $ _____

2
```
   5,782
     491
 +    69
_____
```

3 How many lines of symmetry could you draw on the figure below?

○ 3
○ 2
○ 1

4 Round 369.2284 to the nearest thousandth.

_____

5 Madison wants to plant tulips in her garden in patterned rows. Each row will have 12 tulips in a repeating pattern of red, yellow, yellow, white. If Madison plants 8 rows of tulips, how many of each color will she need?

_____ red   _____ yellow   _____ white

1 $98,234 - 998 = $ _____

2
$$1\frac{1}{5} \qquad 9\frac{1}{5}$$
$$-\frac{3}{5} \qquad -\frac{3}{5}$$

3 Mark the rule for the pattern.

3 6 4 8 6 12 10 20 18 36 34

○ +3, −2   ○ ×2, ÷2   ○ ×2, −2

4 How many fourths are in six-eighths? _____

5 Ben's dad uses three 14-gallon tanks of gas a month driving to and from his job. What is the average number of gallons he uses per day in a 30-day month?

_____

Show your work.

1. $902 \times 0.08 =$ _____

2. $\begin{array}{r} 8.34 \\ \times\ 0.5 \\ \hline \end{array}$

3. List the numbers in order from smallest to largest.

   91.7   17.9   197   0.791   7.19

   _____ _____ _____ _____ _____

4. A square is a rectangle.

   ○ **yes**   ○ **no**

5. Our parakeet, Tweety, eats one ounce of birdseed each day. About how many weeks will a five-pound bag of birdseed last?

   _____

1. $81 \div \frac{1}{9} =$ _____

2. $22\overline{)8{,}030}$

3. Draw a right triangle.

4. $7^2 =$ _____

5. Members of the school band are required to practice twenty-five minutes every night. About how many hours does a band member practice weekly?

   ○ 2 hours   ○ 4 hours
   ○ 3 hours   ○ 5 hours

Daily Math Practice • EMC 6715 • © Evan-Moor Corp.

➤ **Activity 1**

Farmer Brown built a fence around his henhouse.
He used eight fence posts spaced evenly apart
and one roll of chicken wire.

How far apart were the fence posts?

_____

How long was the roll of chicken wire?

_____

Show your work.

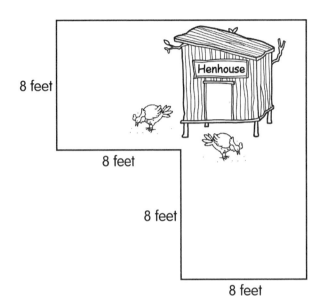

8 feet

8 feet

8 feet

8 feet

➤ **Activity 2**

Read the description and then draw the polygon. Label the length of each side
on your drawing.

- It is a quadrilateral.
- Its perimeter is 16 centimeters.
- It has no right angles.
- It has 2 pairs of congruent,
  parallel sides.
- The lengths of all the sides are
  prime numbers.

1   783 + 348 + 106 = _____

2   $149.08
   + 326.14
   _____

3   If each triangle in the figure is equilateral, what is the perimeter of the figure?

3 in.

_____

4   $8^3 =$ _____

5   Besides spectators, the capacity limit of Victory Stadium includes players, news reporters, and stadium workers. How many nonspectators could be at a sold-out game?

Capacity Limit	42,500
General Admission Seating	31,750
Reserve Seating	10,475

_____

1   8,241 – 3,687 = _____

2   $29.00
   – 4.99
   _____

3   What is the value of z in the equation 4 x 2 – z = 7?

z = _____

4   Mike can do 126 sit-ups in six minutes. How many sit-ups is that per minute?

_____

5   If each rain gauge measures six inches of rainfall, about how much was the total rainfall from Sunday through Tuesday?

Sunday   **Monday**   **Tuesday**

_____

1 249 x 481 = _____

2　　2.5
　　x 0.0 6
　　_____

3 Shade the parts to show $\frac{4}{3}$.

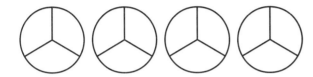

4 Circle the number that is a common multiple of 6 and 8.

15　　68　　24　　90　　32

5 A one-way trolley ticket to Old Town costs $3.50. How much will it cost for Diego and three friends to ride to Old Town and home again?

$_____

---

1 $\frac{1}{12}$ ÷ 6 = _____

2 15)$\overline{123,045}$

3 If the sum of two numbers is 15 and the product is 56, what are the two numbers?

_____ and _____

4 Volume is measured in square units.

○ **yes**　　○ **no**

5 A one-gallon can of paint costs $17.00. A one-quart can costs $4.39. Which is the better buy?

○ gallon can　　○ quart can

Show your work.

➤ **Activity 1**

Arrange the numbers **4**, **8**, **12**, **16**, **20**, **24**, **28**, **32**, and **36** so that the sum of each diagonal line is **100**.

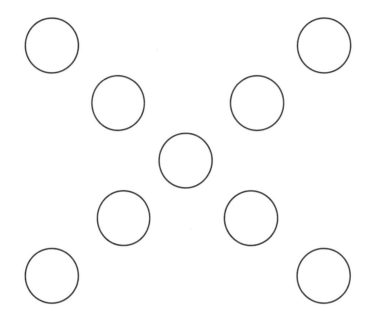

➤ **Activity 2**

Write the digits 1 through 9 on the lines to complete the equations. Use each digit only once.

_____ + _____ = 10

_____ − _____ = _____

_____ × _____ = 8

_____ ÷ _____ = 3

1   2.37 + 82.9 = _____

2   10,948
    – 6,819

3   What is the value of *n* in the equation?

    24 + n + 3 = 88

    n = _____

    Show your work.

4   List all the factors of 24.

    _____

5   Will cut open and flattened a box for recycling. Which shape was the box before it was flattened?

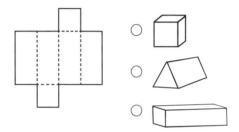

1   $\frac{3}{4} + \frac{1}{2} + \frac{5}{8}$ = _____

2   $9\overline{)7.2}$

3   How many ounces are in 13 pounds?

    _____

4   Write 4,801 in expanded form.

    _____

5   It takes Alice one hour to walk to her grandmother's house. She walked ten minutes and then stopped for a soda. After walking another fifteen minutes, she stopped for an ice-cream cone. She walked fifteen more minutes after that and then stopped to visit Mrs. Smith. What fraction of the trip had Alice completed by then?

    ○ $\frac{2}{3}$ ○ $\frac{3}{4}$ ○ $\frac{5}{6}$

1   80,192 x 0 – 34 = _____

2 $2\frac{1}{8}$
    $+ \quad \frac{3}{5}$
    _____

3   Jenna needs $\frac{1}{2}$ yard of material to make one placemat. If she has 5 feet of material, how many placemats can she make?

_____

4   Reduce $\frac{36}{42}$ to simplest form. _____

5   Circle the **first** number that is incorrect in the solution to this problem.

$$
\begin{array}{r}
4\,6\,1,5\,9\,2 \\
\times \qquad 3\,0\,8 \\
\hline
3\,5\,9\,2\,7\,3\,6 \\
1\,3\,9\,4\,7\,7\,6\,0 \\
\hline
1\,4\,2,0\,7\,0,3\,3\,6 \\
\end{array}
$$

1   5.34 ÷ 4 = _____

2
100	1,000	10,000
x 357	x 357	x 357

3   What is the least common multiple (LCM) of 2, 6, and 8?

_____

4   What comes next?

8   4   10   6   12   8   _____

5   Luke and Joshua ordered an extra-large cheese pizza with pepperoni on only one-third of it and sausage on only one-fourth. If the pizza was cut into twelve slices, how many slices were just plain cheese?

_____

➤ Activity 1

Mrs. Shelton doesn't have enough green and red markers for everyone in her class. Every two students share a green marker, and every four students share a red one. If Mrs. Shelton has fifteen green and red markers in all, how many students are in her class?

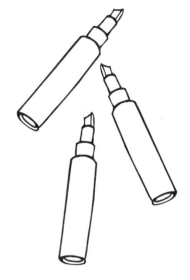

_____

➤ Activity 2

How many problems can you solve in one minute?

21	56	47	18	30	19	72	63
+34	+12	+52	+40	+67	+40	+28	+95

68	43	97	54	29	85	27	76
−24	−12	−63	−20	−15	−51	−11	−33

15	22	36	47	51	60	74	83
x 2	x 3	x 1	x 0	x 4	x 5	x 8	x 6

5)55 6)24 7)56 8)72 9)45 10)40 11)99 12)84

_____ correct

1 $12^2 =$ _____

2
```
  9.5        4.5
x 4.2      x 9.2
```

3 Write 75.9 in word form and expanded form.

_____

_____

4 Circle the median in this set of numbers.

4   7   9   10   5   12   6

5 Jorge is making nachos for six people. The recipe calls for three cups of cheese. How much cheese would Jorge need to make nachos for two dozen people?

_____

Show your work.

1 $4 \div 5 =$ _____

2
```
  2,468
x    60
```

3 Write the correct symbol in the circle.

$3\frac{3}{4} + 2\frac{1}{2}$ ◯ $10.75 - 4.5$

4 3 : 15 :: 60 : _____

5 Sarah's baby brother Jesse weighed 8 pounds 3 ounces when he was born. Now Jesse weighs 12 pounds. How much weight has he gained?

_____

1 1,073 ÷ 37 = _____

2 $2\frac{3}{4}$
      $+\,4\frac{1}{6}$
   _____

3 What is the volume of the cube?

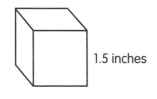

1.5 inches

_____

4 What is 50% of 20? _____

5 Half of the fruits in the bowl are apples and one-third are bananas. All the rest are oranges. What fraction of the fruits are oranges?

_____

Show your work.

---

1 95 ÷ 5 = _____

2 $3\frac{3}{4}$
      $-\,2\frac{2}{5}$
   _____

3 Write the number below in standard form.

six hundred six and six hundredths

_____

4 If $a = 4$ and $b = 2$, then $3a + 3b =$ _____.

5 The school band had a doughnut sale to raise money for new uniforms. Band members baked 6,000 doughnuts to sell for $7.00 a dozen. If they sell all the doughnuts, how much money will they have for uniforms?

$_____

Show your work.

> ## Activity 1

1. Plot the following ordered pairs on the grid: (6, 5) (5, 1) (2, 1) (3, 5)

2. Draw lines to connect the points. What shape do they create?

    _____

3. Mark the point that is 5 below and 6 to the left of (2, 1). What are its coordinates?

    _____

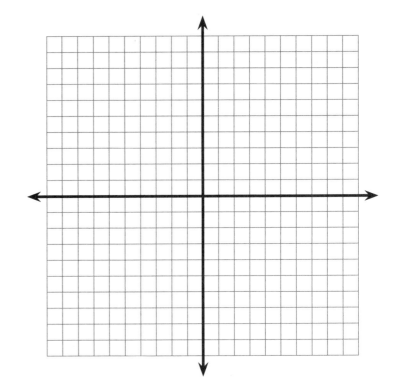

> ## Activity 2

1. Plot the points below on the grid. Then connect the points.

    (6, 4) (−2, 4) (6, −4) (−2, −4)

2. Mark the center point of the figure you created. What are its coordinates?

    _____

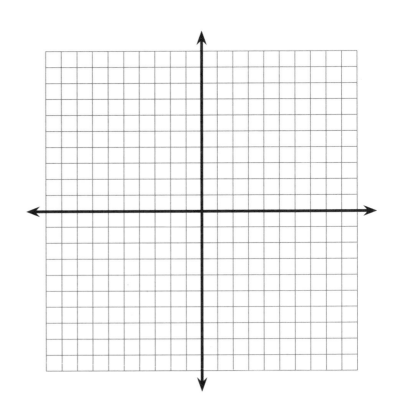

1   666 ÷ 9 = _____

2
$$\begin{array}{r} 346 \\ \times\ 64 \\ \hline \end{array} \qquad \begin{array}{r} 346 \\ \times\ 6.4 \\ \hline \end{array}$$

3   How many minutes are in $3\frac{5}{12}$ hours?

_____

4   Mark the rule for the pattern.

322   32.2   3.22   0.322

○ +10   ○ ÷10   ○ ×10

5   Logan's watch has a 90-day warranty. If the watch stops working six weeks after Logan bought it, is it still under warranty?

○ **yes**   ○ **no**

Show your work.

---

1 $\frac{1}{2} \div \frac{1}{2} =$ _____

2
$$\begin{array}{r} 6.21 \\ \times\ 35 \\ \hline \end{array}$$

3   If $a = 110$, then $a \times 0 =$ _____.

4   Round 92,187,999 to the nearest hundred thousand.

_____

5   Kylie is on a swing. The swing moves back and forth twice every five seconds. About how many minutes will it take Kylie to go back and forth one hundred times?

○ $3\frac{1}{2}$ minutes

○ 4 minutes

○ $4\frac{1}{2}$ minutes

1 7.6 + 0.18 = _____

2 −4 + 5 = _____

3 What is the best estimate for 197 x 21?

○ 4,000   ○ 4,500   ○ 5,000

4 2^3 = _____

5 Toshi has six coins that total 91 cents. How many of each coin does he have?

_____ quarter

_____ dime

_____ nickel

_____ penny

_____ half dollar

1 897,412 + 34,879 = _____

2
$$497{,}002 \atop -\ 36{,}284$$ $$497.002 \atop -\ 36.284$$

3 Write 57.3 in word form.

_____

4 List all the factors of 16.

_____

5 Ava has 80 pictures to put in her photo album. She can fit 4 photos on each page of the album. If the album has 15 pages, does Ava have room for all her photos?

○ **yes**   ○ **no**

Why or why not?

_____

_____

The top four players on the soccer team scored 100 goals this season. Dylan scored 35 goals. Mason scored 20 goals. Savannah scored 15 goals. Lydia scored 30 goals. Complete the table to show each player's goals as a fraction (in simplest form) and as a percent.

	goals	fraction	percent		goals	fraction	percent
Dylan	35			Savannah	15		
Mason	20			Lydia	30		

Make a circle graph to show the information in the table. Remember to give the graph a title.

1 4,783 + 1,348 + 106 = _____

2
```
  700,300
-  94,082
```

3 Write the numbers in order from smallest to largest.

8.00   8.30   0.800   0.83

_____   _____   _____   _____

4 What is the value of *x* in the equation 2*x* = 368 − 4?

x = _____

5 At the ballgame, Isabelle bought two hot dogs ($2.25 each), two sodas ($1.00 each), and one bag of peanuts ($1.50). If she paid with a ten-dollar bill, how much did she get back?

$_____

1 2(9 × 3) = _____

2
```
  $4.85
-  2.56
```

3 Complete the drawing so that it is symmetrical.

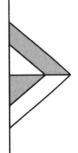

4 Water freezes at 0°C. It is 10 degrees above freezing outside, and the temperature is predicted to drop 16 degrees. What will the temperature be then?

_____°F   _____°C

5 Jayden is thirty years younger than his mom. His mom is two years older than his dad. If his dad is thirty-nine, how old is Jayden?

_____

Daily Math Practice • EMC 6715 • © Evan-Moor Corp.

1 $\frac{4}{7} + \frac{1}{2} + 2\frac{1}{8} =$ _____

2
$$\begin{array}{c} \frac{3}{4} \\ \times \frac{4}{5} \\ \hline \end{array} \qquad \begin{array}{c} 0.75 \\ \times\; 0.80 \\ \hline \end{array}$$

3   What is 20% of 10?   _____

Show your work.

4   Write in word form the value that **4** has in 2.674.

_____

5   Claire is writing a report about kangaroos. The report must be two full pages. If she can fit 20 lines on each page with about 20 words per line, approximately how many words in all will Claire's report be?

_____

1 $\frac{3}{8} + 1\frac{3}{8} =$ _____

2 $39\overline{)8,852}$

3   How many inches are in 7 yards?

_____

4   If $a = 6$, then $2a + 4a \times a =$ _____.

5   Fifteen players, 2 coaches, and 21 parents attended this year's sports banquet. The cost of each meal was $12.00 plus 5% (0.05) sales tax. What was the total cost of food for the banquet?

$_____

Show your work.

1. Shade the boxes with the correct factors.

factors of 12	5	11	7	7	8	11	9	7	13	9	5	7	10	7	3
factors of 41	3	2	10	4	11	5	7	6	12	18	9	18	3	2	1
factors of 60	60	1	5	7	2	12	4	8	3	15	10	9	20	6	30
factors of 48	3	5	12	9	24	7	4	11	16	11	48	10	1	13	2
factors of 72	36	12	72	5	4	3	6	7	18	24	8	10	9	2	1
factors of 19	2	3	19	4	7	11	5	10	5	6	12	9	13	8	8
factors of 16	8	3	2	7	13	3	10	14	6	15	5	11	9	12	6
factors of 24	3	2	8	5	7	9	9	13	5	14	11	19	5	10	7

2. Shade the boxes with the correct multiples.

multiples of 6	25	79	30	15	31	69	17	40	54	35	15	43	72
multiples of 7	41	92	15	101	54	19	111	38	49	66	75	26	91
multiples of 8	39	51	80	95	14	47	76	108	16	94	26	86	72
multiples of 9	96	78	45	69	19	50	21	75	81	48	17	31	27
multiples of 10	18	65	60	93	90	20	70	102	10	30	80	64	50
multiples of 11	33	51	99	23	77	38	44	89	66	101	11	40	62
multiples of 12	72	48	84	35	24	60	96	81	12	108	144	20	36

3. Decode the shaded message. _____

1 13 x 39 = _____

2 $\frac{5}{8} + \frac{3}{4} + \frac{9}{16}$ = _____

3 Write the name of the figure.

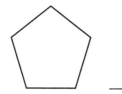

_____

4 What value of x makes the equation true?

$426 - x = 329$ $x =$ _____

5 Twelve students have bikes. Half of the bikes are black. One-sixth of the bikes are silver. One-fourth of the bikes are red, and the rest are blue. How many bikes are there of each color?

black _____   silver _____

red   _____   blue _____

---

1 8.4 ÷ 7 = _____

2   12,345,678
     − 9,876,543
     _____

3 Write the number below in standard form.

six thousand and one hundredth

_____

4 Round 9.098 to the nearest tenth.

_____

5 It takes Owen four minutes to eat eight carrot sticks. How long does it take him to eat one?

_____

1   392.87 − 100.99 = _____

2   $\frac{1}{8}$ $\frac{3}{8}$

   $\frac{2}{3}$ $\frac{1}{3}$

   $+ \frac{1}{6}$ $+ \frac{5}{6}$
   ———   ———

3   Write $3\frac{27}{100}$ as a decimal. _____

4   What are the common factors of 4 and 10?

   _____

5   The bakers at the pretzel shop work eight hours a day. Together, they make ten trays of pretzels every hour, with a dozen pretzels on each tray. How many pretzels in all do they bake a day?

   _____

1   9.9 ÷ 33 = _____

2   900
    × 146
    ———

3   $\frac{1}{3}$ of a dozen eggs = _____ eggs

4   What is the perimeter of the triangle?

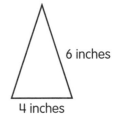

6 inches

4 inches

   _____

5   Mr. Nutty had 100 jars of peanut butter to sell. He sold a dozen jars each day last week. How many jars does he have left?

   _____

➤ **Activity 1**

Write each value in the correct place to show the number in standard form.

8 ones 2 hundreds 3 tenths 6 tens _____268.3_____	5 hundreds 2 tens 7 hundredths 1 tenth 4 thousands _____	6 tens 4 ten thousands 9 hundreds 6 ones 8 hundredths _____
1 hundred thousand 5 tens 9 hundredths 9 tenths 5 ones _____	2 tenths 6 hundreds 3 millions 1 ten thousand 8 tens _____	5 hundredths 4 ones 2 hundreds 8 tenths 6 tens _____

➤ **Activity 2**

Write each number in expanded form.

707.41 _____

8,422.8 _____

586.95 _____

3,023.06 _____

200,977.2 _____

65,012.03 _____

1 9.6 ÷ 20 = _____

2   2,400   2,400
      x   101   x   10.1
     _____   _____

3 The number is between 20 and 40. It is an odd number. Its digits add up to 8. The larger digit minus the smaller digit is 2. What is the number?

_____

4 Which is greater?

○ $6\frac{1}{3}$ ○ 6.3

5 When Jake bought his pet snake, it was 0.87 m long. Now the snake is $1\frac{1}{4}$ m long. How much did the snake grow?

_____

1 $7^2 \times 10^2$ = _____

2 $964 \div \frac{1}{2}$ = _____

3 Which formula should be used to find the area of the figure?

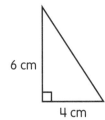

6 cm

4 cm

○ $A = b \times h$

○ $A = \frac{1}{2}l \times w$

○ $A = \frac{1}{2}b \times h$

4 What is the range of the data below?

8, 4, 12, 23, 11, 5, 38, 15, 8, 27, 3

_____

5 Driving to Adam's grandmother's house takes three days and two nights. The trip each way costs $56.00 a day for gas, $47.00 a day for food, and $60.00 a night for lodging. What will the total travel expenses be for the trip there and back?

$_____

1. $-12 + 4 =$ _____

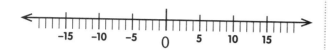

2. 0.37
   × 1.08
   _____

3. Continue the pattern.

   88   44   64   32   52   _____   _____

4. What is the value of b in the equation $9b + 5 = 41$?

   $b =$ _____

5. Eli bought a jacket that was on sale at 40% off. The original price of the jacket was $60.00. How much did Eli pay?

   $_____

1. $3^3 =$ _____

2. $10\frac{1}{10}$
   $+ \ 2\frac{1}{2}$
   _____

3. Which is less?

   ○ $8\frac{1}{8}$ ○ 8.08

4. What is the LCM of 2, 4, and 5?   _____

5. Samantha answered 90% of the questions on her math test and 80% of the questions on her history test correctly. If each test had 50 questions, how many questions in all did she answer correctly?

   _____

   Show your work.

➤ **Activity 1**

How much does one block weigh? _____

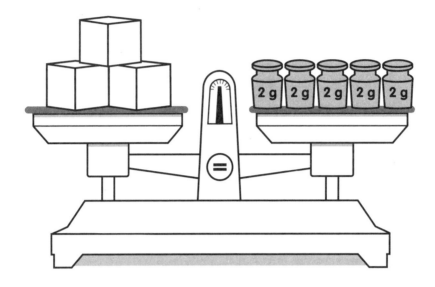

➤ **Activity 2**

Write the improper fraction and the mixed number for each model.

	improper fraction	mixed number

1.
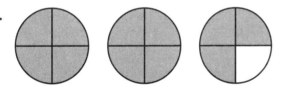

_____ _____

2.
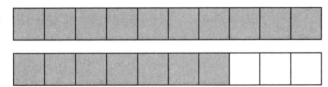

_____ _____

3.
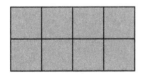 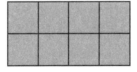 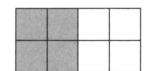

_____ _____

1 $10^3 =$ _____

2 $2^4 =$ _____

3 Which weight is greater?

　○ 0.001 kilograms
　○ 10 grams

4 What is the GCF of 25 and 41? _____

5 If Paul saves $3.00 every week for twelve weeks and then buys a CD for $15.00 plus 9% tax, how much money will he have left?

$_____

Show your work.

---

1 $-2 + -5 =$ _____

2 $-20 + 15 =$ _____

3 Write four numbers that are less than 5 and greater than 3.

_____ _____ _____ _____

4 Continue the pattern.

72　86　75　89　80　_____　_____

5 Anneke's science class measured ten inches of rainfall during the month of May. What was the average rainfall per day? (Round your answer to the nearest hundredth.)

_____

1 $\frac{1}{6} \times \frac{4}{5} =$ _____

2 $3\frac{1}{3}$
$+1\frac{1}{4}$
———

3 Write an expression for the phrase below.

80% of a number is 60

_____

4 If $z = 3$, then $(9 \times 5) + z = 48$.

○ **yes**   ○ **no**

5 Peter grew an average of $\frac{1}{2}$ inch a month last year. If he was 4 feet 6 inches tall at the beginning of the year, how tall was he at the end of the year?

_____

Show your work.

---

1 $-10 + 3 =$ _____

2 $-3 - 6 =$ _____

3 Round 88,855 to the nearest hundred.

_____

4 List all the factors of 18.

_____

5 The soccer team played a total of twenty-four games and won four more games than they lost. What was the team's win–loss record for the season?

wins _____   losses _____

➤ **Activity 1**

Write the ordered pair for each point on the coordinate grid.

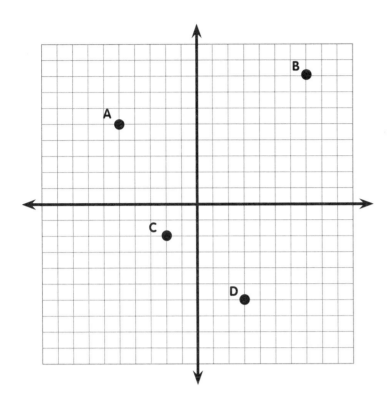

A _____

B _____

C _____

D _____

➤ **Activity 2**

Follow the rule to complete each function table.

Rule: ÷ $\frac{1}{3}$	
Input	**Output**
3	9
6	
9	
12	
15	
18	

Rule: x0.25	
Input	**Output**
3	0.75
6	
9	
12	
15	
18	

1 $(18 + 7) - 10 =$ _____

2 $8^5 =$ _____

3 Find the area.

$7\frac{1}{2}$ feet

$3\frac{1}{4}$ feet

_____

4 Write 210% in decimal form. _____

5 Thirty students are at soccer practice. Each group of three students needs a soccer ball and two field cones. How many balls and cones are needed in all?

_____ balls   _____ cones

---

1 $8\frac{2}{3} + 6\frac{1}{5} =$ _____

2 60% of 20 = ?

◯ 1,200   ◯ 12   ◯ 120

3 Create a number pattern for the rule **x2, +10**.

8 _____ _____ _____ _____

_____ _____ _____ _____ _____

4 Draw an **X** on the figures that are congruent.

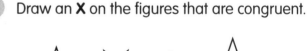

5 Jo is supposed to read half of a 100-page book for her English assignment. She has finished 38 pages. What percent of the assignment does she have left?

_____

1   89,002 x 386 = _____

2   25)$38.25

3   What does one-half of three and two-thirds equal?

_____

Show your work.

4   If $a - b = 9$ and $a = 36$, then $b =$ _____.

5   The school parking lot has room for thirty cars. If only six spaces are empty, what fraction of the parking lot is in use?

_____

If Mrs. Johnson parks in an empty space, how does the fraction change?

_____

_____

1   0.06 x 78 = _____

2   −10
       +   7
       _____

3   Which of these angles is less than 90 degrees?

   ○ obtuse   ○ acute   ○ right

4   Estimate 21 x 297. _____

5   Seiko has 7 coins that add up to $1.10. She has the same number of quarters as dimes. The rest of the coins are nickels. How many of each coin does she have?

_____ quarters

_____ dimes

_____ nickels

A **palindrome** is a number that is the same read either backward or forward. The number **2332** is an example of a palindrome.

To find out if a number can become a palindrome, add the number to its reverse. If it is not yet a palindrome, reverse the sum and add it to the answer. Continue reversing and adding until the answer becomes a palindrome.

Example: 57 + 75 = 132 (**132** is <u>not</u> a palindrome.)

132 + 231 = 363 (**363** is a two-step palindrome because it goes through two reversals before the sum becomes a palindrome.)

Circle the numbers that are **two-step** palindromes: 32   48   50   64   76   82   91

Work Space

1   8,465 − 2,681 = _____

2
$$\begin{array}{r} \$14{,}490.08 \\ +\ \ \ 3{,}276.15 \\ \hline \end{array}$$

3   What solid figure will this pattern make?

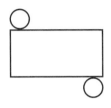

_____

4   88% of $33.00 = _____

5   Write the missing operation sign in each shape to find the answer to the last equation. (Each shape represents only one sign.)

If 31 ◯ 2 ◯ 3 = 186 and

13 ☐ 4 ☐ 2 = 7 and

128 ▽ 52 ▽ 20 = 200,

then 5 ◯ 3 ☐ 12 ▽ 8 = _____.

1   Estimate the answer.

1,389 ÷ 73 = _____

2
$$\begin{array}{r} 27\frac{3}{4} \\ -\ 19\frac{1}{3} \\ \hline \end{array}$$

3   What is the LCM of 3, 7, and 2?

_____

4 10^4 is more than 1,000.

◯ **yes**   ◯ **no**

5   Emma weighed 6 pounds 9 ounces when she was born. Her weight doubled by the time she was six months old. How much did she weigh then?

_____

1   297,450 − 691 = _____

2   $\begin{array}{r} 3.02 \\ \times\ \ 0.9 \\ \hline \end{array}$

3   What comes next?

1,000   100   10   _____   _____

What rule does the pattern follow?

_____

4   What solid shape is a basketball?

_____

5   Six more than eight times a number equals thirty. Write the equation.

_____

What is the number?   _____

1   $\begin{array}{r} 8,263,145 \\ +\ 1,097,688 \\ \hline \end{array}$

2   $72\overline{)3,672}$

3   What solid shape is a brick?

_____

4   List all multiples of 8 that are less than 100.

_____

5   The plumber charged Mrs. Evans $225.00 for materials and $35.00 an hour for labor to fix her leaky sink. The total bill came to $347.50. How many hours did it take the plumber to fix the sink?

_____

➤ **Activity 1**

David's garden produced six bushels of zucchini, three bushels of beans, seven bushels of corn, and four bushels of beets. In the table below, write the fraction (in simplest form) and the percent of David's total crop that each vegetable represents.

Show your work.

vegetable	fraction	percent
beans		
beets		
corn		
zucchini		

➤ **Activity 2**

Write the fraction (in simplest form), decimal, and percent for the shaded part of each grid.

1.
2.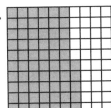
3.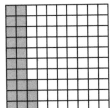
4.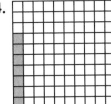

1. fraction _____
   decimal _____
   percent _____%

2. fraction _____
   decimal _____
   percent _____%

3. fraction _____
   decimal _____
   percent _____%

4. fraction _____
   decimal _____
   percent _____%

1. 340 x 0.034 = _____

2. Correct any errors.

    14,687
    − 9,781
    ────────
     5,308

3. Write the factors of 28. Circle the prime factors.

    _____

4. Round 699.6 to the nearest whole number.

    _____

5. The sunglasses that Ramon wants to buy are 50% off the original price of $85.00. If he also has to pay 6% sales tax, what will be the total cost of the sunglasses?

    $_____

    Show your work.

1. 7.05 − 3.93 = _____

2. 24)‾5,832‾

3. Write five million two hundred eighty in standard form.

    _____

4. Circle the composite numbers.

    92   59   23   47   78   19

5. David has two pet mice. Together, the mice eat $\frac{1}{2}$ cup of dry food pellets every week. How much dry food will David need to feed his mice for one year?

    _____

    Show your work.

1 30 + 10 − 9 = _____

2   −17
     + 11
     ‾‾‾‾

3 Which solid figure has one triangular base and three triangular faces?

   ○ triangular prism
   ○ triangular pyramid

4 What are the common factors of 14 and 35?

   _____

5 Arrange the numbers **2**, **4**, **6**, **8**, and **10** in the circles so that the numbers added either vertically or horizontally equal **18**.

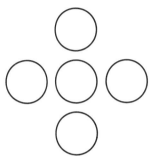

---

1 $1\frac{3}{4} \div 2 =$ _____

2   10.05
     + 5.2
     ‾‾‾‾‾

3 What is the area of a right triangle that has sides measuring 10 cm, 15 cm, and 18 cm?

   _____

4 $1^3 \times 628 =$ _____

5 When Sasha traveled from San Francisco to Boston, the plane took off at 11 a.m. Pacific Time and landed at 7:30 p.m. Eastern Time. With the three-hour time difference between California and Massachusetts, how long was Sasha's flight?

   _____

1. What is the name of the tool that is used to measure angles?

   ○ prism   ○ polyhedron   ○ protractor

2. Measure each angle and write the number of degrees.

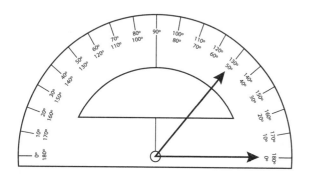

_____ degrees

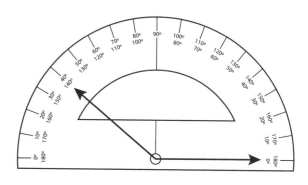

_____ degrees

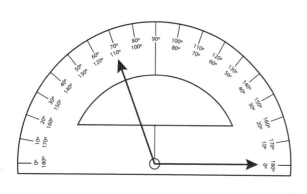

_____ degrees

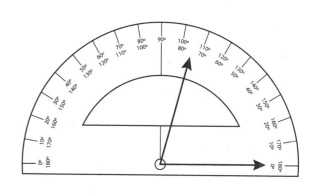

_____ degrees

3. Draw a right angle.

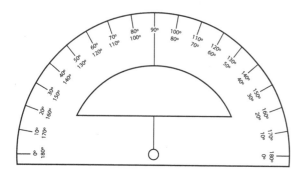

4. Draw a 45° angle.

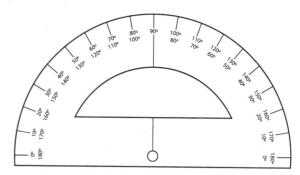

1 $42 + 3^4 =$ _____

2      $3\frac{2}{3}$
       $4\frac{1}{4}$
    $+ 5\frac{3}{5}$
    _____

3 Write six million four hundred thousand six and six hundredths in standard form.

    _____

4 If $x \div 5 + 8 = 15$, then $x =$ _____.

5 The pirate captain ordered his men to dig for treasure. Six men dug, one at a time, in equal shifts for a total of three and a half hours. How long was each man's shift?

    _____

    Show your work.

1 $\frac{2}{7} \times 4\frac{1}{2} =$ _____

2   0.5
    $+ 0.15$
    _____

3 What is the sum of the angles in a triangle?

    _____ degrees

4 How many inches are in $15\frac{1}{2}$ yards?

    _____

5 Patrick left home at 4:20 p.m. on Sunday. He returned 36.3 hours later. What day and time was it when he got home?

    _____

    Show your work.

1. $(-4) + (-8) = $ _____

2.
$$\begin{array}{r} 50{,}027 \\ \times\ \ \ 0.27 \\ \hline \end{array}$$

3. What is the measurement of the third angle of a triangle if the other two angles each measure 45 degrees?

   _____

4. What is the GCF of 15, 33, and 54? _____

5. Greg wants to divide a block of cheese that weighs $2\frac{1}{2}$ pounds into four equal pieces. How many ounces will each piece weigh?

   _____

   Show your work.

1. $7.5 \times 0.8 = $ _____

2.
$$\begin{array}{r} 7\frac{1}{2} \\ \times\ \ \frac{4}{5} \\ \hline \end{array}$$

3. Continue the pattern.

   44   1   55   2   66   3   77   _____   _____

   _____   _____   _____   _____

4. Which is greater?

   ○ 5,000 decimeters

   ○ 0.51 kilometers

5. Twenty percent of the students at Taft Middle School play in the band. If the band has forty members, how many students attend Taft Middle School?

   _____

The dice below show different views of the dots on each cube.

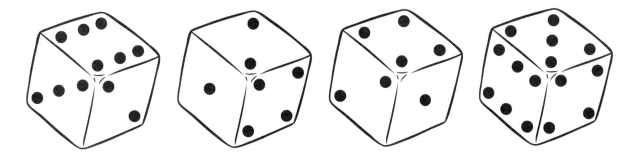

1. How many dots are on the side opposite **6**? _____

2. How many dots are on the side opposite **4**? _____

3. How many dots are on the side opposite **2**? _____

4. Draw the missing dots on the dice below.

1 $15^2 =$ _____

2 $7\overline{)2.38}$ $70\overline{)2.38}$

3 What is the smallest fraction you can write using the digits 2, 3, and 4? (Use all three digits in your answer.)

_____

4 What is the area of the parallelogram?

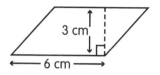

3 cm

6 cm

_____

5 Rob's height is $\frac{2}{3}$ of his dad's height. If Rob's dad is 6 feet 3 inches tall, how tall is Rob?

_____ feet _____ inches

1 $9,000 \times 0.01 =$ _____

2 Use the distributive property to write the expression another way.

$4 \times (8 + m)$

_____

3 Write 78.2 in word form.

_____

4 How many cups are in 1.5 gallons?

_____

5 What is the ratio of w's to **all** consonants in the following sentence?

Wes and Willow went for a walk.

_____

1. $734 + 821 + 486 + 999 = $ _____

2. $\begin{array}{r} 0.1 \\ \times\, 0.01 \\ \hline \end{array}$

3. What is the perimeter of a pentagon if each side measures 31 feet?

_____

4. Round 87.395 to the nearest hundredth.

_____

5. When the queen counted her jewels, she found that she has five pearls, two opals, and three rubies for each diamond and two emeralds for each opal. If the queen has three diamonds, how many jewels does she have altogether?

_____

1. $\frac{1}{2}$ of $724 = $ _____

2. $\begin{array}{r} \frac{9}{10} \\ \frac{9}{100} \\ + 9\frac{9}{1,000} \\ \hline \end{array}$

3. List all the factors of 21.

_____

4. Write the next two numbers in the sequence.

$\frac{1}{2}$ $\frac{1}{4}$ $\frac{1}{8}$ _____   _____

5. Sofia has 7 coins that total 68 cents. What coins does she have?

_____

_____

> ## Activity 1

The chart below shows the amount of time Austin spent working out at the gym last week.

Day	Number of Minutes
Monday	45
Tuesday	50
Wednesday	36
Thursday	70
Friday	49

1. What is the total amount of time Austin worked out? (Round your answer to the nearest hour.)

_____

2. What is the average amount of time Austin worked out each day?

_____

> ## Activity 2

Every day, Ella practices piano half as long as she practices gymnastics. She takes half an hour to eat dinner and watches television twice that long. She does homework for an hour more than she practices gymnastics and two hours more than she watches television.

Complete the chart to show how much time Ella spends on each activity.

Activity	Number of Minutes
piano	
gymnastics	
dinner	
television	
homework	

1   606.06 x 2 = _____

2   88$\overline{)118.8}$

3   What is 5% of 240? _____

Show your work.

4   169 : 13 :: 36 : _____

5   To earn money, Bryan mows lawns every Saturday. He is paid $15.00 a lawn. If he mows seven lawns each Saturday, how many weeks will it take him to earn $1,000.00?

_____

Show your work.

1   541.8 ÷ 84 = _____

2 $98.89
   +   0.62
    —————

3   If 16x equals 4, what does x equal?

    ○ 4   ○ 0.4   ○ $\frac{1}{4}$

4   What is the measurement of the fourth angle of a quadrilateral if the other angles measure 60°, 120°, and 90°?

_____

5   Pedro needs nine hours of sleep a night. If he has to be up at 5:30 a.m., at what time should he go to bed?

_____

1 $20^3 =$ _____

2 $\begin{array}{r} -4 \\ + \; -7 \\ \hline \end{array}$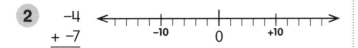

3   If an angle measures 110°, what kind of angle is it?

○ acute

○ obtuse

○ straight

4   In the number 698.713, which digit is in the hundredths place?

_____

5   Devin caught two trout that each weighed 2 pounds, a sunfish that weighed 8 ounces, and a catfish that weighed 12 ounces. What was the average weight of the fish that Devin caught?

_____

1 $777.55 \div 5 =$ _____

2 $\begin{array}{r} 3\frac{5}{7} \\ + \; 9\frac{2}{3} \\ \hline \end{array}$

3   A line is perpendicular to another line when the lines intersect at right angles.

         ○ **yes**   ○ **no**

4   How many square yards of carpet should Stella order if her bedroom measures nine feet by twelve feet?

_____

5   The number has two digits. It is greater than thirty but less than fifty. It is an odd number. The sum of the digits is ten. What is the number?

_____

➤ **Activity 1**

1. Write the fraction under each figure to show equivalents.

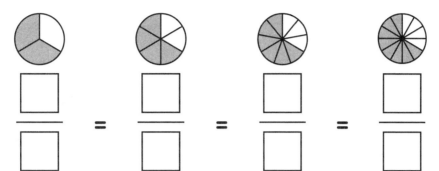

2. Divide and shade each rectangle and fill in the missing numerator to show equivalent fractions.

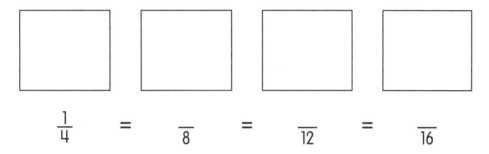

$$\frac{1}{4} \quad = \quad \frac{}{8} \quad = \quad \frac{}{12} \quad = \quad \frac{}{16}$$

➤ **Activity 2**

Convert each improper fraction to a mixed number and each mixed number to an improper fraction.

$\frac{28}{7} =$ _____ $\frac{33}{15} =$ _____ $8\frac{2}{3} =$ _____

$\frac{49}{9} =$ _____ $3\frac{7}{12} =$ _____ $\frac{57}{13} =$ _____

$12\frac{3}{10} =$ _____ $10\frac{9}{16} =$ _____ $\frac{96}{10} =$ _____

1 126 x 0.67 = _____

2 $\frac{5}{6} \div 5$ = _____

3 One number is incorrect in the solution below. Find the number and circle it.

$$
\begin{array}{r}
1,392 \\
\times \quad 37 \\
\hline
9744 \\
4176 \\
\hline
50,504
\end{array}
$$

4 The numbers 48 and 63 have two common factors. What are they?

_____ and _____

5 John gave his friend Sam $\frac{1}{4}$ of his marbles. Sam lost three of the marbles, so now he has only five. How many marbles did John have to start with?

_____

1 −14 + 22 = _____

2 $3\frac{1}{8}$
$\times 1\frac{1}{4}$

3 Continue the pattern.

31 5 32 10 33 15 _____ _____ _____

4 $\frac{3}{8}$ of 16 = _____

5 Tosha swims on a four-person relay team. If each person on the team swims two lengths of a 100-yard pool in each relay, how many relays will the team have to complete to swim a total distance of at least one mile? (1 mile = 5,280 feet)

_____

Show your work.

1   348.54 ÷ 37 = _____

2   3.21
   x 5.07
   ——————

3   List the factors of 32.

_____

4   Reduce $\frac{51}{57}$ to simplest form. _____

5   Tyler ran a half marathon (approximately 13 miles) and completed the race in one hour and forty-four minutes. What was his average running time per mile?

       about _____

---

1 100^4 = _____

2   51.32
   31.76
  + 27.02
   ——————

3   10% of 54 = _____

   60% of 54 = _____

   Show your work.

4   What is the area of the triangle?

17 cm   _____

       8 cm

5   Chloe the cat uses 5 pounds of kitty litter every two weeks. If her owner buys a 5-kilogram bag, about how long will it last? (1 kg = approximately 2.2 lbs.)

      _____

Match each net to its three-dimensional figure.

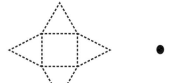

•   •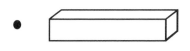

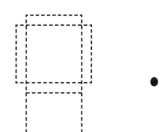

•   •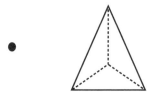

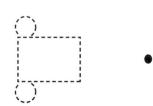

•   •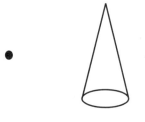

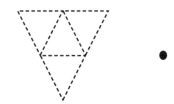

•   •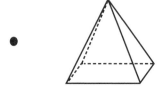

•   •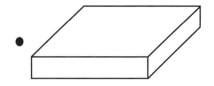

•   •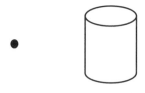

1   96.24 ÷ 2 = _____

2   0.03   0.3
    x   0.2   x 0.2

3   Jalil asked for two triple-dip ice-cream cones. If each single-dip cone costs $1.69, and each extra scoop of ice cream is 85¢, how much will he have to pay?

         $_____

4   Lines AB and CD are ____.

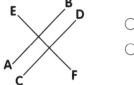

   ○ parallel
   ○ perpendicular

5   Lines CD and EF are ____.

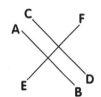

   ○ parallel
   ○ perpendicular

1 $4\frac{2}{3} \times 3\frac{4}{9}$ = _____

2   0.3 $0.3\overline{)7.5}$
   x 7.5

3   What kind of angle is CAB?

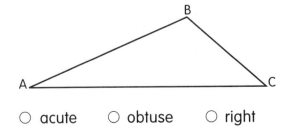

   ○ acute   ○ obtuse   ○ right

4   Reduce $\frac{36}{144}$ to simplest form.   _____

5   Zach's dad will travel from Boston, MA, to Richmond, VA. The trip is about 600 miles. About how fast will Zach's dad have to drive to get there in $10\frac{1}{4}$ hours?

       about _____ mph

Show your work.

1 725,649 + 583,129 = _____

2 36,000 – 98.2 = _____

3 Write the algebraic expression for the following phrase.

a number plus 8 minus 10

_____

4 Circle the equilateral triangle.

5 Mrs. Roberts has organized her class into 4 teams. Each team has the same number of students. Boys make up $\frac{3}{4}$ of each team, and there are 2 girls on each team. How many students in all are in the class?

_____

1 654,201 – 498,999 = _____

2 $25\overline{)37{,}192}$

3 Which is heavier?

○ 1,000 milligrams
○ 10 grams

4 If $0.3x = 2.4$, then $x =$ _____.

5 Jennifer mixed 4 tablespoons of frozen concentrate with $\frac{3}{4}$ cup of cold water to make one 8-ounce serving of orange juice. How many cups of orange juice will Jennifer be able to make with a 12-ounce can of frozen concentrate? (2 tbsp. = 1 ounce)

_____

Show your work.

The Summer Sports baseball club sold pizzas to raise money for new equipment and uniforms. The club treasurer used a **line plot** to keep track of the number of pizzas sold in each order.

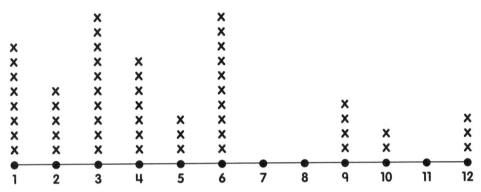

Number of Pizzas per Order

1. How many orders were taken in all? _____

2. How many pizzas were sold in all? _____

3. If the pizza prices were $5.00 each, 3 for $13.00, and 6 for $24.00, what was the total amount of money earned from orders of each quantity? (Make sure you give each customer the best pricing.)

Number of pizzas per order	1	2	3	4	5	6	9	10	12
Total amount of sales	$40.00								

Work Space

1 0.21 x 7.03 = _____

2 9,765,945
   + 282,067
   _____

3 Mark all the shapes that always have only two sets of parallel sides.

○ rhombus   ○ trapezoid

○ square   ○ parallelogram

4 Round 967,727 to the nearest hundred thousand.

_____

5 Anthony bought two shirts at a special sale. He paid the full price of $19.99 for one shirt and got a second shirt of the same price for half off. If the sales tax rate is 8.5%, how much sales tax did Anthony pay for the two shirts?

$_____

1 $\frac{1}{4}$ x 640 = _____

2 $43\overline{)28,036}$

3 The baseball game started at 2:15 p.m. and lasted 2 hours and 48 minutes. At what time did the game end?

_____

4 What are the range and the average for this set of numbers?

6.2 8.1 7.4 3.5

range _____

average _____

5 Stavros ordered a pizza for $5.99, a soda for $1.50, and breadsticks for $2.49. If he gives the cashier a ten-dollar bill, how much change will he get back?

_____

1 $9\frac{5}{9} \div \frac{1}{9} =$ _____

2   76,321
        x 3,748

3 If two angles of a triangle measure 45 degrees and 71 degrees, what is the measurement of the third angle?

_____

4 Mark and label −1, −2$\frac{1}{2}$, and $\frac{3}{4}$ in the correct positions on the number line.

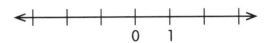

5 A rancher has 500 cattle grazing in the pasture. When his cowhand rides into the pasture on horseback to round up the cattle, how many legs are in the pasture?

_____

1 $50^3 =$ _____

2   −2   −2
       + 6   + −6
      _____   _____

3 How many inches are in $6\frac{3}{4}$ yards?

_____

4 $\frac{1}{4} : \frac{3}{4} :: 75 :$ _____

5 Popeye the parrot can sing three notes— C, E-flat, and G. List all the different tunes he can sing using all three notes. Each tune can use each note only once.

_____   _____

_____   _____

_____   _____

_____   _____

_____

Claire's family is moving, and she needs to pack her 15-volume set of encyclopedias. Each book in the set measures 10 x 8 x 1.5 inches. Claire has four empty boxes, but she wants to pack all 15 volumes in no more than two boxes. How many volumes of Claire's encyclopedias will fit in each box below? Circle the two boxes that, together, will hold all of Claire's encyclopedias.

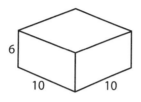

_____ volumes

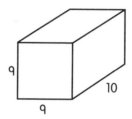

_____ volumes

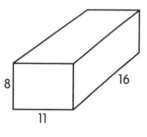

_____ volumes

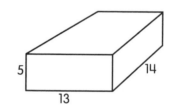

_____ volumes

Work Space

1 $86.4 \div 2.5 =$ _____

2 $9\frac{4}{5}$
 $\times\ 3\frac{2}{3}$
 _____

3 Which measurement is the best estimate of a new pencil's length?

 ○ 7 cm ○ 17 cm ○ 170 cm

4 Mark the correct word form of 67.92.

 ○ sixty-seven and ninety-two tenths
 ○ sixty-seven and nine tenths and two hundredths
 ○ sixty-seven and ninety-two hundredths

5 If Jason ran 1.8 miles and Josh ran 3,200 yards, who ran the farthest? (1 mile = 5,280 feet)

 _____

1 $(3 - 4) + 6 =$ _____

2 Is the answer correct? ○ **yes** ○ **no**
 If **no**, correct any errors.

  2,964
  + 1,043
  _____
  3,907

3 How many quarts are in 6.8 gallons?

 _____

4 What is the smallest fraction you can write using the digits 6, 7, and 1?

 _____

5 Grace's bag of gumdrops has three purple candies, six orange candies, four yellow candies, and one green candy. If Grace reaches into the bag without looking, what is the chance that she will pull out a yellow candy?

 _____

1   564.02 x 3.5 = _____

2   Use the distributive property to rewrite the expression 3(4 + *n*).

_____

3   What is the perimeter?

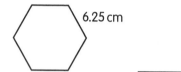

6.25 cm

_____

4   How many cups are in a gallon?

_____

5   Bubble gum comes in packs of 7 pieces and cases of 48 packs. If Teera needs 7,500 pieces of bubble gum for a carnival, how many cases should she order?

_____

1   6.43 ÷ 0.5 = _____

2
      54,968,432
       3,135,978
  +   824,721
  _____

3   What is the ratio of *s*'s to all letters in the sentence?

     She sold six sea stars.

_____

4   If 7*x* = 441, then *x* = _____.

5   Aiko and Amy had a lemonade stand. They started with 3 gallons of lemonade. At the end of the day, they had 1.5 quarts left. How many 8-ounce glasses of lemonade did they sell?

_____

➤ Activity 1

1. Plot and label the coordinate pairs for points **A**, **B**, **C**, and **D** on the grid.

   A (3, 1)   **C** (−2, 3)
   B (4, 6)   **D** (−5, 2)

2. Name the ordered pairs for points **E**, **F**, **G**, and **H** on the grid.

   E _____   G _____

   F _____   H _____

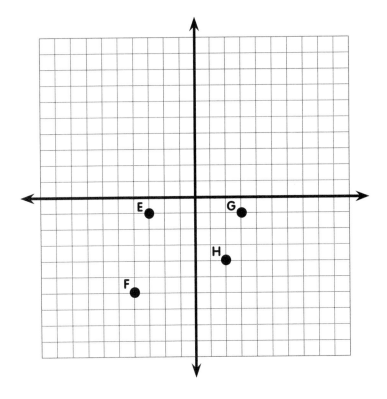

➤ Activity 2

Write the number on the line, and then make a dot on the number line and label it to show that value.

1. the opposite of +2   _____

2. half of $1\frac{1}{2}$ _____

3. 2.5 − 3.25   _____

4. $-2\frac{7}{8} + 1\frac{3}{8}$ _____

1 $9.23 \div 71 =$ _____

2
$$9.23 + 0.71$$ $$9.23 + 0.071$$

3 $4^3 =$ _____

$4^4 =$ _____

$4^5 =$ _____

4 How many milliliters are in one liter?

○ 10   ○ 1,000

○ 100   ○ 10,000

5 If there are sixty-four knives, forks, and spoons on the table and each place setting has two forks, how many places are set?

_____

1 $296 \times 3.04 =$ _____

2 $15\overline{)21}$ $15\overline{)210}$ $15\overline{)2,100}$

3 What is the area?

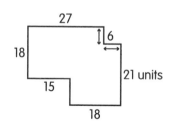

_____

4 $61\frac{4}{7} - 35\frac{1}{2} =$ _____

5 If each person at a picnic drinks 710 milliliters of soda, how many two-liter bottles are needed for 10 people?

_____

1 $127\frac{3}{8} - 44\frac{1}{4} =$ _____

2 $904.34 + 135.97 - 855.86 =$ _____

3   Find the area.

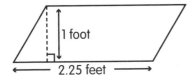

1 foot

2.25 feet

_____

4   Circle the fractions that are expressed in simplest form.

$$\frac{19}{77} \qquad \frac{34}{51} \qquad \frac{8}{13} \qquad \frac{16}{48} \qquad \frac{28}{112}$$

5   Tia wants to sew a patchwork quilt. She wants the finished size of the quilt to be 81 x 110 inches. She will use 6-inch squares cut from eight different fabric patterns. If Tia wants about the same number of squares in each pattern, approximately how many squares should she cut from each different fabric?

_____

1 $5\overline{)11.35}$ $0.5\overline{)11.35}$

2
$$\begin{array}{r} 4.03 \\ \times\, 2.71 \\ \hline \end{array} \qquad \begin{array}{r} 0.403 \\ \times\, 0.271 \\ \hline \end{array}$$

3   What is •———————• ?

         A   B

    ○ line

    ○ ray

    ○ line segment

4   Fill in the missing numbers.

_____   9   11   33   35   105   107   _____

5   A televised football game that lasted a total of three hours had commercial breaks every ten minutes. Each break aired one 60-second commercial and three 30-second commercials. What percentage of the game's total air time was used for commercials?

_____

➤ **Activity 1**

Write an expression that shows how to solve each problem.

Problem	**Expression**

1. Gina has 4 pairs of shoes. Her older sister has x more pairs. How many pairs of shoes does Gina's older sister have?

_____

2. Henry had n errors on his spelling test. His friend Hannah misspelled twice as many words. How many words did Hannah spell wrong on the test?

_____

3. Anthony's mom is h inches tall. Anthony is 14 inches shorter. How tall is Anthony?

_____

4. Maria bought t roses so that she can make identical Mother's Day bouquets for her mom and her two grandmothers. How many roses will Maria use for each bouquet?

_____

5. Pui baked z dozen fortune cookies. She gave away $\frac{2}{3}$ of them to friends and neighbors and kept the rest for her family. How many fortune cookies did Pui keep for her family?

_____

6. Kyle usually spends $\$d$ on a bag of dog food, but when it's on sale for 20% off, he buys 2 bags. How much does Kyle usually spend when he buys 2 bags?

_____

➤ **Activity 2**

Evaluate the expression for each variable.

$n =$	$n \times 10$
7	
24	
3	
100	
66	
18	

$n =$	$n \div 10$
50	
680	
10	
320	
45	
97	

$n =$	$\frac{1}{2}n$
34	
120	
68	
2	
0.6	
99.8	

How to Solve
Word Problems

 Read the problem carefully. Think about what it says.

 Read the problem again and look for clue words. They will tell you which operation to use. Below are some examples of clue words.

 Solve the problem. **Hint:** Sometimes you will use more than one operation.

 Check your work. Does your answer make sense?

Clue Words

Add	Subtract	Multiply	Divide
in all	more than	times	parts
altogether	less than	product of	equal parts
total	are left	multiply by	separated
sum	take away	area	divided by
both	difference	by	quotient of
plus	fewer	(with measurements or dimensions)	a fraction of
			average

Place Value Chart

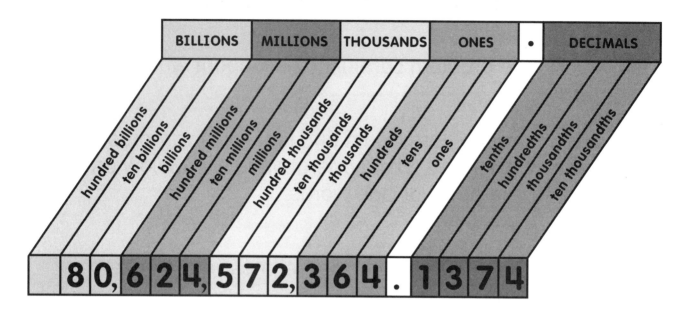

Fahrenheit and Celsius Chart

Fahrenheit	Celsius
212°F	100°C
225°F	110°C
250°F	120°C
275°F	135°C
300°F	150°C
325°F	160°C
350°F	180°C
375°F	190°C
400°F	200°C

Daily Math Practice • EMC 6715 • © Evan-Moor Corp.

Congratulations!

_____

(name)

You have successfully completed your math practice!